Trains of America

By Donald J. Heimburger

All-color railroad photography featuring the late steam and early diesel era

Printed in Hong Kong

HEIMBURGER HOUSE PUBLISHING CO.
7236 W. Madison St.
Forest Park, Illinois 60130

DEDICATION

This book is dedicated to my brother and two sisters—John, Louise and Ruth—all of whom have graciously tolerated my railroad habit and even encouraged me with it over the years.

Acknowledgements

For *Trains of America*, I was fortunate enough to know friends who were able to supply color slides and transparencies from their collections. These people gladly loaned their color pictures to allow me to present a wide variety of railroads and color schemes within the time period from about 1940 to 1965.

Without their help, this book would have taken much longer to produce. I'm very grateful for their valuable assistance. They are:

Richard Bowers
Chris Burritt
Jerry Carson
Norton Clark
FJC Products
Lawson Hill
Owen Leander

Bob Nicholson
Leon Onofri
Bill Raia
Brad Smith
Robert Stonich/Rail Photos Unlimited
Richard Wallin
Charles Zeiler

Library of Congress Catalog Card Number: 89-84380
ISBN: 0-911581-13-8

First Edition
Printed in Hong Kong

Heimburger House Publishing Company
7236 West Madison Street
Forest Park, Illinois 60130

Contents

Introduction
Those fascinating trains of America

Many of you have lived during the final days of steam locomotives on America's railroad. You may not remember much from those days, such as specifics of what was happening in the railroad industry at that time, but you probably have retained some general impressions as I did.

One impression that comes to mind instantly for me is seeing the long coal drags, headed by a steam locomotive, on the *Main Line of Mid-America*, the Illinois Central, charging through Tolono, Illinois where I grew up. The IC coal trains were very loud and often disrupted the free movies I went to see as a youth in downtown Tolono. That's the only recollection of steam in my early days. Steam locomotives were nearly gone in the '50s, but I do remember the Wabash's blue, white and gray F7 diesels and the IC's classy chocolate brown and yellow E unit diesels heading up passenger trains traveling to and from New Orleans.

The '50s were a special time for many of you, I'm sure. They were impressionable years, especially when it came to trains. Perhaps you rode many trains, like I did, over such routes as the Denver & Rio Grande Western, the Santa Fe, the Baltimore & Ohio or the Burlington. Or maybe you remember going down to the local railroad station in town and waiting for a train to come by, or maybe you knew the schedule for certain trains and went down to "meet" the train.

NEW MOTIVE POWER

In any case, one of the bright spots for me was seeing a new piece of motive power roll by with a new paint scheme or a recently outshopped unit with a fresh coat of paint. I also looked for multiple lashups between Alco, GE, EMD and Baldwin units. Running these units together in the same train was always interesting to me and added intrigue in my mind as to what the superintendent of motive power for that railroad was thinking when he assigned those locomotives to that train.

Many of the railroads that were in operation in the 1950s and into the mid-60s are no longer with us; they've been merged or purged from the scene. Looking back, I'm surprised at the number of railroads still operating in 1965 that today have disappeared, at least in name. The giant New York Central and Pennsylvania railroads are gone in name. Ann Arbor, Erie-Lackawanna, Chesapeake & Ohio, Atlantic Coast Line, Western Pacific, Milwaukee Road, Great Northern and Burlington are gone. Smaller lines have vanished, too, such as the Lehigh Valley, Chicago & Eastern Illinois, Chicago Great Western, and Wabash.

Baltimore & Ohio #5660, a T-4a with large 73″ drivers and 240 pounds of steam pressure, highballs a freight through town. *J. Schmidt, collectin of Owen Leander*

A look at the May, 1965 *Official Guide of the Railways* is both educational and interesting. The number of name passenger trains operating in the United States was impressive, even for that late date. The Chicago & North-Western still featured several "400" trains between Chicago and Green Bay; the Southern Pacific sponsored the streamliners *Sunset* and *Golden State* between Chicago and Texas; the Soo line operated the *Winnipeger* between St. Paul and Winnipeg; the Richmond, Fredericksburg & Potomac ran several trains between New York and Washington, D.C.; the Atlantic Coast Line ran Pullman, coach and dining car service on the *Everglades* between New York and Washington; and the Frisco's passenger trains consisted of the *Will Rogers, Meteor* and others.

Even the Chicago Great Western *(The Corn Belt Route)* operated Trains #13 and #14 between Minneapolis-St. Paul and Omaha-Council Bluffs. The Katy ran the *Texas Special* between Kansas City and Dallas, featuring "friendly, attentive service in an atmosphere of restful comfort."

'GOOD OLD DAYS'

Those were the "good old days" of railroading in my youth that I remember, and I suspect they were good days for you, too.

Trains of America recalls the earlier days when steam locomotives were riding their last rails in the United States and when diesels were beginning to appear. We looked with some sadness as the steam-driven iron horse disappeared, but we were also excited about the numerous variations of types and paint schemes the diesels ushered in. Many of those early diesels have now disappeared as well, and we've forgotten the beauty of their gleaming, streamlined profiles.

Trains of America recaptures a period of tremendous change on our nation's railroads; it does it in large, sweeping color photographs that befit the grandeur of railroads in our country. This book rekindles our love for the trains of America and shows how they operated and how they looked some 40 years ago and as recently as 20 years ago.

I've included photographs of many different kinds of trains in this book, both freight and passenger, as well as some 85 different railroads and transit systems in America. To a large degree they represent the American railroad system as it was operated at the time. I've even included photographs from the Canadian Pacific and the Canadian National railroads for variety.

This book represents hundreds of hours of photography time through the years by the various rail photographers who traveled thousands of miles to obtain the photos you see here. For them it was a labor of love that induced them to spend time capturing the American rail scene of years ago.

I hope you'll spend hours engrossed in this color book, remembering your youth and the trains you saw then, or remembering another time in your life when trains played an important part in your activities. Passenger trains especially, I believe, bring us good memories because of the people we meet on board and the adventure of travel itself. My own love of the trains of America can best be summed up in that poem that goes:

My heart is warm with the friends I make,
and better friends I'll not be knowing.
But there isn't a train I wouldn't take
No matter where it's going.

Donald J. Heimburger
September, 1989

New York Central E8 at Worcester, Mass. *Brad Smith*

The huge steam locomotive drivers are a reminder that the iron horse once ruled the rails. *Chris Burritt*

Ann Arbor

With its Halloween orange paint still bright, an Ann Arbor 1,000-hp RS-1 pushes freight cars onto the Lake Michigan ferry *City of Milwaukee* in 1975 at Frankfort, Michigan. From Frankfort, the Ann Arbor car ferry operated to Menominee and Manistque, Michigan, and Kewaunee and Manitowoc, Wisconsin. The spark arrestor on the road switcher is in compliance with Michigan state laws. Note the extra gyrating headlight below the main headlights. These units were once painted in the parent Wabash colors of gray, blue and white. *Brad Smith*

Ann Arbor caboose #2846 receives some attention in the Owosso, Michigan shops on February 5, 1976. The bright red sides and cupola, silver roof and brilliant yellow ends (when new) made these tail-end cars easily seen. Ann Arbor, once controlled by the Wabash, was incorporated in 1895 and in 1973 went into bankruptcy; in 1976 Conrail took over. *Collection of Don Heimburger*

Arcade and Attica

Ex-Escanaba & Lake Superior #14, a 4-6-0 built by Baldwin in 1917, proceeds toward the highway crossing at Curriers, New York, on another passenger-carrying run of the Arcade & Attica in 1982. The common carrier line, which dates back to 1881, uses passenger cars from the Delaware, Lackawanna & Western. The quiet beauty of rolling hills, blue sky and white clouds forms a picturesque backdrop for #14 on this summer day. *Don Heimburger*

Atchison, Topeka & Santa Fe

Black with white zebra stripes, this lone 1,000-hp RS-1 built in 1947 by Alco-GE sits patiently in Santa Fe's Chicago yards for its next assignment. #2399 was one of a group of RS-1's the Santa Fe was still running in the middle of 1973. *Brad Smith*

The striking red, yellow and silver warbonnet paint scheme that Santa Fe applied to its streamlined locomotives was a symbol of all that Santa Fe's passenger service stood for: fast schedules, elegant, clean cars and fine dining. Here an F7A leads four more F7s in a sight that, unfortunately, is not to be repeated again. The year is 1965, and the "golden age" of streamlined passenger service will come to an abrupt halt in 1971 when Amtrak takes over the nation's passenger trains. *Chris Burritt*

Whether on the road traveling at 65 miles an hour or in the yard catching their breath, Santa Fe's passenger F7s were a delight to behold. Spotting them among other, more drab-colored equipment, was uplifting and encouraging. They literally sang out "come ride with me!" *Brad Smith*

ABOVE. Here #2399, shown on page 7 in zebra stripes, is in new, distinctive blue and yellow dress—and getting *that* cleaned as well! It's 3:55 p.m. on July 25, 1965, and we're in Santa Fe's coach yards in Chicago. RIGHT. McPherson, Kansas on a hot, humid August, 1965 day entertains a visit from #2675, a 1,500-hp GP7; the locomotive does switching duties on this Florence to Garden City, Kansas line. *Both photos, Chris Burritt*

A pair of colorful yellow and blue Fairbanks-Morse H16-44's containing 1,600 horsepower each bask in the sun on this bright September day in 1965. The units had already been serving Santa Fe for 13 years when this photo was shot. *Chris Burritt*

Nos. 2675 and 2893, both GP7's and both built in the early 1960s, huddle together at McPherson, Kansas during switching maneuvers. *Chris Burritt*

Apparently fresh from the paint shop, #2398 switches the Santa Fe coach yard in Chicago in July of 1965. The 1,000-hp Alco-GE RS1, built in 1947, had been renumbered in May 1949. *Chris Burritt*

NEXT PAGE, TOP. Locomotive #279C, an F7, and a B unit, tag along behind a Santa Fe FA unit, helping roll a freight train across prairie rails in the mid-60s. BOTTOM. Military cargo is carried by this freight passing through New Mexico and led by a quartet of F units, including #253C and #238C. *Both photos, Chris Burritt*

An RSD5 built in 1953 by Alco-GE, accompanied by a few more crew members than necessary, couples onto a caboose during work chores. *Chris Burritt*

Built in 1949 as a Santa Fe business car and a duplicate of the *Santa Fe* built for the chief executive officer of the road, the *Atchison* was a streamlined open platform beauty. The two large windows in the observation lounge area at the rear of the car provided great views. Remote control radio equipment was situated in the car, plus the usual speed and air gauges for the benefit of whatever official was riding in the car. Even the rear platform was fluted. *Chris Burritt*

This is a Santa Fe color line-up that you'll probably never see again, unless it's in a railroad museum. Fairbanks-Morse #519, a 1,200-hp H12-44 built in the early 50s, is flanked by a sister unit on its right. Behind, another H12-44 in zebra stripes adorns the rails, and in the rear, the classic silver, red and yellow F unit shouts out the traditional SF passenger car colors. The date is June 5, 1965 at Corwith Yards in Chicago. *Charles Zeiler*

Aurora, Elgin & Fox River

LEFT AND BELOW. The Aurora, Elgin & Chicago (later the Chicago, Aurora & Elgin), was incorporated in 1901 and in four years had extended its service over tracks of the Metropolitan West Side Elevated, terminating at a station on Wells Street in Chicago's Loop. Samuel Insull sought and got control of the line in 1926 and had big plans for the CA&E which evaporated with the Depression. On noon July 3, 1957 passenger service ended, with freight service following two years later. By mid-1961, the line was abandoned. The AE&C had headquarters in Wheaton, Illinois. The line is remembered today at the Fox River Trolley Museum in South Elgin. *Both photos, Chris Burritt*

Baltimore & Ohio

Pristine Baltimore & Ohio 2-8-2 Mikado #4622 of the series #4600-4634 Class Q-4b takes water at Wildwood, Pennsylvania on June 15, 1955. While hauling a freight here, the Q-4b's could be used in passenger service because of their steam heat and air signals. During World War II they pulled hundreds of troop trains. By 1959 all had been regulated to the scrap line. *Jerry Carson*

In 1942, 14 years prior to this picture, B&O #5306, a 4-6-2 Pacific, was converted from a P-7 to a P-7b. The Pacific locomotive was the workhorse of the B&O passenger fleet, the first going into service as early as 1906. In 1956, Jerry Carson was trackside in Chicago to record this picture on a cold, winter February day.

#5070 of the P-1d Class, this high-stepping Pacific with 74″ drivers, gets ready to haul another passenger train. Note the large square tender which could hold 21 tons of coal and 13,500 gallons of water—the engines were the most powerful Pacifics the B&O owned. *Jake Schmidt, collection of Owen Leander*

ABOVE. Big Mountain type 4-8-2, a Class T-3a with 70″ drivers and built by the B&O in 1943, is ready to pound the crossover with its 187 tons of weight, giving anyone nearby a grand symphony of harmonious complexity as steel hits steel. #5564 was built by B&O's Mt. Clare shops to help with war traffic. *Jake Schmidt, collection of Owen Leander*

RIGHT. A 2,250-hp E8 #1449 of 1953 shows its blue and gray coloring with yellow accent stripes. B&O purchased 16 of these units of the PE-5 Class from EMD. *Brad Smith*

B&O and C&O trains congregate at New York's Grand Central Station in this February 27, 1966 photo. Numberboards lit and logos in tact, B&O and C&O passenger trains are on their last journies through America under their own sponsorship. But you could still take B&O trains such as the *Ambassador*, the *Cincinnatian*, the *Columbian* and the *Capitol Limited*. *Charles Zeiler*

The date is September 25, 1955 and the B&O was running excursion trains such as this one growling near Blairs Corner, Pennsylvania. The FA's with white flags waving were a sight to behold. *Jerry Carson*

Bangor & Aroostook

Bangor & Aroostook owned eight of the odd-looking BL2's made by EMD in 1949. Here, #51 with 1,500-hp rests at Millinocket, Maine. Originally Nos. 550-557, they were later changed to Nos. 50-57. *Brad Smith*

Boston & Maine

RIGHT. The tracks fight with tall and growing weeds for space in this tranquil scene on the Boston & Maine, with #1225, a 1,200-hp SW9 and crew setting out cars. *Brad Smith*

A 1,500-hp F3A, built in 1948, emerges from the greenery around Bellows Falls, Vermont on Boston & Maine right-of-way. Bellows Falls is on the B&M's Springfield to White River Junction line. *Brad Smith*

Canadian National

ABOVE. Jasper, Alberta, Canada is a spectacular spot for scenery, as well as train-watching. Here Canadian National #9000, an F3A, idles along with other locomotives that sport the green and yellow paint scheme. *Brad Smith*

RIGHT. A GP9 trundles past a switch tower with a local freight drag at Port Arthur, Ontario. The outside-braced box car second from the engine recalls days of railroading past when these cars were commonplace. *Brad Smith*

ABOVE. An FP9 leads three more CN power units—including two Geeps—along the tracks through Edmonton, Alberta and past a row of now-extinct 40-foot box cars. *Brad Smith*

LEFT. Two RDC cars pause at Edmonton for rest and reloading before continuing on their way. The air-conditioned RDC's were named *Railiners* and the CN was called "The Way of the Worry Free." *Brad Smith*

Canadian Pacific

ABOVE. Three Geeps and an F unit bring power to the rails at Calgary, Alberta, Canada. The maroon, gray and yellow-striped diesels are guided by #8668, a GMD-built GP9 constructed in 1957. In freight service, it was rated at 1,600-hp. *Brad Smith*

RIGHT. Gleaming in the morning sun, Canadian Pacific #1421 FP7 and sister unit glide through Montreal, Quebec with a long passenger train. "The World's Most Complete Transportation System" had general offices at Windsor Station in Montreal. *Brad Smith*

Central Vermont

Train Nos. 76-59 and 66-75 were the CV's *Ambassador*, the Montreal to New York train that left Montreal at 10:50 a.m. and arrived in New York's Penn Station at 11:20 p.m. The *Ambassador* is at Swanton, Vermont. *Richard Wallin*

Central of New Jersey

RIGHT. A Central of New Jersey RDC takes a breather at Communipaw, New Jersey while a Reading 1,500-hp FP7 #902 peeks its head around the corner. *Brad Smith*

PRECEDING PAGE. Train action in earlier days on the 367-mile Central Vermont Railway looked like this. Owned by the Canadian National, the CV's general manager operated the line from offices at St. Albans. The #4550 is a 1,750-hp GP9 hauling an extra (note white flags) near Norwich, Connecticut. *Brad Smith*

ABOVE. This 1954-built Trainmaster H24-66 rolls its four-car load through Elizabeth, New Jersey on the Jersey Central Lines. *Brad Smith*

Chatahooch

LEFT. The Chattahoochee Industrial Railroad, operating 15.4 miles from Hilton to Saffold, Georgia hauls pulpwood, wood chips, steel and chemicals. RS1 smokes it up doing daily chores. *Brad Smith*

Chesapeake & Ohio

ABOVE. Engine #1169, a husky light Mikado of the K-2 Class was delivered to the Chesapeake & Ohio from Richmond in 1924. The engine had Baker valve gear, 63" drivers and a length over couplers of more than 88 feet. It featured a Vanderbilt tender that held 12,000 gallons of water and 15 tons of coal. *Jake Schmidt, collection of Owen Leander*

RIGHT. A combination of a C&O F7A, and B&O FB and FA-2 units are used to haul a C&O freight train in this colorful action scene taken in June of 1965 by photographer Brad Smith.

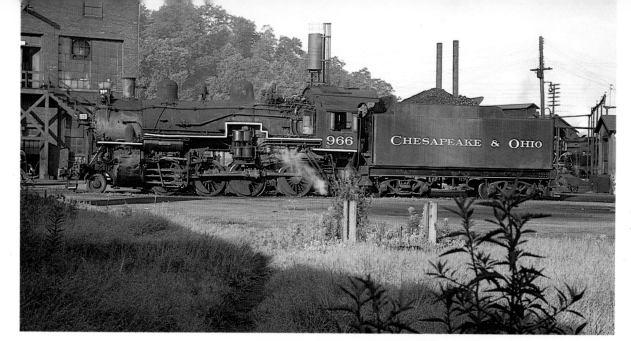

A Class G7 2-8-0 simmers peacefully in the morning sun while this coal-hauling railroad goes about its varied tasks on other parts of the C&O property. #966 also operated at Illinois Central's Chicago terminal in 1946—C&O used the terminal, too. Engine #966, built in 1903, subsequently was superheated. *Jake Schmidt, collection of Owen Leander*

Locomotive #3007 and sister unit, in the C&O's public relations-directed blue and yellow color scheme, are about three years old in this picture, having been new in 1962. On later GP-35 units the "bulge" over the cab disappeared with newly-designed electrical controls. *Chris Burritt*

In May of 1966, C&O's E8 #4020, one of the first diesels on that road's Chesapeake District used in passenger service, is seen traveling through Williamsburg, Virginia with some more varnish. In May of 1951, the C&O ordered 27 EMD E8's like this, each rated at 2,250-hp. *Brad Smith*

C&O #7057, an F7, and a B&O diesel, pause alongside GM&O #801A, an F3, and a B unit at Springfield, Illinois on January 4, 1964. C&O's #7057 nose is becoming chipped, but that's no particular sign of financial deterioration. It's the GM&O that will seek the financial safety of merger with the Illinois Central in 1972. The C&O and the B&O today, however, are combined, as C&O controls B&O and has since 1963. *Richard Wallin*

Chicago Transit Authority

It's a warmish June day in 1965 as a two-car Ravenswood train on the Chicago Transit Authority line heads toward the stop at the Merchandise Mart north of the Chicago River and Chicago's famous Loop. Immediately to the south of the river, the Lake-Dan Ryan line crosses these tracks. To the left of the on-coming train was where North Shore interurban trains terminated on their runs between Milwaukee and Chicago. *Chris Burritt*

Chicago & Illinois Western

Illinois Central's own Chicago shortline, the Chicago & Illinois Western, was piloted during the early 60s by IC head man Wayne A. Johnston, who acted as president of that road, too. The line ran from Western Avenue in Chicago's Brighton Park area to the suburb of Willow Springs. The road, about six miles in length, also ran north to IC's Hawthorne Yard. #101 was an SW7 built in 1950. *Richard Wallin*

Chicago & Western Indiana

Here on April 11, 1965, Chicago & Western Indiana's 1,000-hp Alco-GE RS1 (built 1949) lugs passenger cars near Chicago's 47th Street. Later, the unit was sold to Genessee & Wyoming. *Charles Zeiler*

Chicago, Milwaukee, St. Paul & Pacific

The Milwaukee Road, *Route of the Hiawathas.* The Milwaukee, one of the most prosperous forward-looking railroads at the turn of the century. In 1929 it operated over 3,074 miles of track. In 1979, 3,064 miles of track. Engine #100C is an FP7. *Chris Burritt*

LEFT. #96C departs Milwaukee in October of 1964. *Brad Smith*

ABOVE. On the *Hiawathas*, the famous Skytop Lounge was the place to be and be seen—and to watch the scenery. One of four parlor-observation cars to be built by the Milwaukee in 1948 exclusively for the *Hiawatha* trains, the *Cedar Rapids* was a fitting end car to an impressive train. *Brad Smith*

RIGHT. Take your pick of the *Morning* or *Afternoon Hiawatha* with Skytop Lounges, or the *Pioneer Limited* with duplex roomettes, roomettes and double bedrooms, or Trains No. 55 and 56, or Train 58 with reclining seat lounge coaches; travel on the Milwaukee Road in 1966 *still* wasn't distasteful. *Brad Smith*

In the summer of 1930, the Milwaukee had 14 daily trains from Milwaukee to Chicago *alone;* there were even more trains that ran daily except Sundays and on alternate days. Then there were the long-distance passenger trains, some operated by the *numbers,* others with names like *The Southwest Limited, The Columbian, The New Arrow* and even *The Fisherman* (Chicago to Star Lake with observation sleeping cars and standard 10 section-2 compartments-drawing room cars). Here, 35 years later at Milwaukee, glides one more train movement, keeping the rails shiny. *Brad Smith*

Engine #32C, an E9, beckons her long yellow string of passenger cars out onto the main line Milwaukee Road tracks from her namesake's passenger terminal. It's July 1965. *Brad Smith*

ABOVE. A 1,200-hp Fairbanks-Morse diesel switcher with silver trucks and extended window on the cab tows box cars around Milwaukee in July of 1965. *Brad Smith*

A 1,000-hp Fairbanks-Morse #760 and helper #691, a 2,400-hp TR4 calf unit, move past the camera lens with a transfer caboose and under telltails. Date: August, 1965. *Brad Smith*

ABOVE: *"America's Longest Electrified Railroad—656 Miles of Transcontinental Line Now Operated by 'White Coal.'"* So reads a 1930s Milwaukee Road public timetable. A total of 656 miles of line was electrified in the 30s. On a very snowy April 27, 1958 in Butte, Montana, E-2, a bi-polar electric, brings the *Olympian* into town. *Richard Wallin*

Two RSC2s and an RSD5 attack the Viroqua, Wisconsin branch of the Milwaukee Road on April 8, 1972. *Richard Wallin*

NEXT PAGE. Milwaukee train station, September, 1966. *Chris Burritt*

ABOVE. The locomotives were always there—lined up like in a parade, waiting for the on-lookers and railfans. Bensenville, Illinois' Milwaukee Road engine servicing facility was located adjacent to a public road, as shown. And as such, there was an unobstructed view of the likes of Fairbanks-Morse #27C. *Charles Zeiler*

Two FP7's start their run to DePue, Illinois at Ladd on October 25, 1978. Never mind the fading orange and yellow-turned-almost-white paint. *Bob Nicholson*

The fireman peers out the cab window of his F7 to wait for the highball sign at Savannah, Illinois inbound to Chicago in 1965. *Chris Burritt*

Orange and black Geeps await the call to work at Savannah, Illinois on March 21, 1981. Note the old-fashioned roundhouse doors to the right. *Bob Nicholson*

Chicago, Rock Island & Pacific

The Rock Island's Chicago terminal—LaSalle Street Station—bids welcome to all weary travelers. The clock shows 1 p.m., and in a couple of hours the Chicago commuter rush will begin and the station will fill. *Charles Zeiler*

An Alco-GE 1,600-hp RS3 sends smoke signals out to clear the right-of-way ahead at Englewood Station, Chicago on April 11, 1965. The #490 spent 17 years serving The Rock and was eventually traded in to GE. It was part of the last 15 RS3's used in suburban service exclusively, and featured a steam boiler, 80 mph gearing and h.e.p. generator. *Charles Zeiler*

Sometimes called "the E6B with a view," the Rock Island's #750 is a bizarre-looking piece of motive power, but the RI never seemed to let that bother them. It and sister #751 were to be used as a second unit on the *Rocky Mountain Rocket.* When the plan was scrubbed, they went to work pulling bi-level commuter trains out of Joliet. Here it's leaving LaSalle Street Station, Chicago in May of 1965. *Brad Smith*

One of the three EMD ultralight train experiments of the 1950s, the LWT-12 *Jet Rocket* was delivered to the Rock Island in January of 1956 but didn't live up to even suburban service expectations: they were noisy, and they didn't roll smooth. Thus, 10 years after being delivered, with a short stint in *Rocket* service, #2 was disposed to the National Railway Museum in Green Bay, Wisconsin. *Charles Zeiler*

Five years after being built and delivered, #630, an E6, looks as good as new at 47th Street in Chicago. The engine was the final pre-war passenger diesel in revenue service in the U.S. It was preserved by the Kansas City Railway Museum in 1979. *Charles Zeiler*

BL2 #429 patiently waits beside an RS3 in May of 1965 in Chicago, one month before being traded to EMD, along with four other BL2's, all delivered in 1948 and '49. They worked for the Rock in local passenger and Chicago suburban service. *Brad Smith*

One of Rock Island's GP18's in the intermediate color scheme, and flanked by a Geep in the newer paint scheme, are running on the Manly to Burlington, Iowa line. The line served nearly the entire depth of the state of Iowa, from north to south, running through West Liberty and Cedar Rapids. *Bob Nicholson*

This outside-braced caboose sits forlornly at Utica, Illinois in April of 1976, its paint taking a beating from railroad service and Mother Nature. *Bob Nicholson*

All the GP35's—34 of them—were received in mid-1965, and they all were delivered with the solid maroon paint scheme with three decal heralds. #331 is shown with a painting variation—white safety stripes on the nose and no herald. *Chris Burritt*

ABOVE. Train #8 at Joliet, Illinois, the Chicago to Denver *Rocky Mountain Rocket,* has left Denver the day before at 11:30 a.m. and is nearing Chicago 40 miles to the east. The spaces in the coaches, parlor cars and sleepers were reserved in advance of departure. Photographer Jerry Carson caught the gleaming hulk of #655 on July 31, 1971.

"Yellow Wings" was the name applied to this Rock paint scheme. The F7 guides a freight through St. Paul, Minnesota in 1970, but the #120 was often used on a pool run with the Penn Central and found in Elkhart. *Jerry Carson*

ABOVE. Engine #403 could be getting ready to haul one of the secondary Rock Island passenger trains such as the *Cherokee*, or the extra-fare train *Golden State* or possibly even a suburban train. The 400 Class of FP7's were used for all these classes of service. *Charles Zeiler*

#430 was the first Rock Geep in the original red and black paint scheme without safety stripes on the ends. Next unit up the ladder, #431 is shown here in 1964, 14 years after delivery, in the maroon and yellow stripe scheme, punched up by the classy-looking silver trucks. This is Ainsworth, Iowa on a summer day. *Jerry Carson*

A fast westbound freight, led by #270 U28B, rounds the curve at Bureau Junction where the Peoria branch leaves the main line. The branch, the first one west of Chicago, is one of many that split from the Rock's main as she spins her web out to the coast, eventually ending at San Francisco. *Bob Nicholson*

The color schemes of diesels on the Rock Island were numerous, and often no one scheme was totally present in any particular train. Two schemes are represented here, and surprisingly, subsequent numbers of diesels as well, the #675 and #676. Bureau, Illinois, December 15, 1978. *Bob Nicholson*

BELOW. Originally #1263, now #4501, this GP7 was part of the ambitious rebuilding program launched by the railroad in 1974 to rectify an increasing number of bad-order units out of service. The date is January, 1976 and the location is LaSalle, Illinois. *Bob Nicholson*

They served the Rock for 25 years and then were traded in to either GE or EMD. The 44-tonners were built by Whitcomb works at Rochelle, Illinois in 1940 and were "let go" in 1965 and 1966. #371 has about a year left before ending her career on the Rock. *Chris Burritt*

Chicago & Illinois Midland

The Illinois Midland, formally the Chicago & Illinois Midland Railway Company, serves the Illinois cities of Peoria, Pekin, Havana, Springfield and Taylorville, cutting its 121-mile route down through the heart of the Prairie State. The freight-service-only road promoted traffic over the line by urging customers to avoid congested terminals to expediate their freight. ''Modern power and equipment guarantee fast and dependable service,'' says the Official Guide. The Powerton, Illinois facility near Pekin shows a couple of SW1200's holing up in September of 1979. *Bob Nicholson*

Chicago Great Western

The Chicago Great Western's route ran from Chicago to Omaha, up to the Twin Cities and down to Kansas City. This 1,000-hp NW2 reflects the line's handsome color scheme as it appeared in 1965. The CGW connected with 56 other railroads along its route. *Chris Burritt*

ABOVE. Is it an Illinois Central or Chicago Great Western GP7? It's CGW, to be sure, but it bears a great similarity to IC's orange, brown and yellow diesels, too. *Don Heimburger*

Even with four major railroads in the Upper Midwest, the CGW was built anyway, starting in St. Paul, Minnesota in 1884. LEFT. The #104A was an F5, shown here at Sycamore under the sanding tower. *Chris Burritt*

Milwaukee, Wisconsin, September, 1966. *Chris Burritt*

Chicago & NorthWestern

ABOVE. Two commuter 4-6-2's, Nos. 583 and 612, begin their daily race from NorthWestern Station in Chicago to the 'burbs in this July 10, 1955 frame. *Jerry Carson*

"All the comforts plus the luxuries." That pretty well sums up life on C&NW's business car #401, found here in the C&NW Station in Chicago on May 19, 1966. Oh, to be a king, or duke or a Railroad President! *Charles Zeiler*

September of 1955 saw the C&NW using 4-6-2's for commuter runs, and a beautiful sight to behold. *Jerry Carson*

C&NW had this F7 in Green Bay, Wisconsin along with some bi-level commuter cars on April 10, 1971. Perhaps it was part of the *Bi-level Flambeau 400. Rail Photos Unlimited*

C&NW #175 4-6-0 at Escanaba, Michigan on November 11, 1957 looks like it is in need of a good washing! Then again, with all that iron ore around the property, what would you expect? *Jerry Carson*

This Fairbanks-Morse unit has a cold weather "blanket" on this, the 7th day of February, 1970. The location is Niagara, Wisconsin which is at the end of the Iron Mountain branch and right across the line from the Michigan state line. *Jerry Carson*

This odd animal is a 1,600-hp Alco-GE RSD5, but it has inklings of also being a FM Trainmaster, at least from this end. C&NW's Omaha, Nebraska rails were hosting the engine on April 21, 1963. *Charles Zeiler*

ABOVE. Two F7's split the work in getting this freight drag over the rails in Chicago in the spring of 1974. *"The Midwest's Finest Freight Service"* was the railroad's motto. Its trackage extended through northwestern Illinois, through Wisconsin, Minnesota, Iowa and South Dakota like a giant web. *Richard Wallin*

There are things worse than switching cars on the C&NW in the Beer City. As the engineer, you may not have gotten such a nicely maintained SW7 such as this. Then again, the C&NW wasn't one for letting their motive power become covered with grime and oil without washing or repainting. *Brad Smith*

51

Loaded with 1,500 horsepower, this C&NW GP7 isn't used to easy work. Give it a string of cars to push or pull and watch it growl off. *Brad Smith*

Here's #1632 again, but this time hauling a transfer freight train to busy Proviso Yard in Melrose Park, Illinois through Oak Park at Ridgeland Avenue. To the right is the Chicago Transit Authority Lake Street line that leads in the distance to the Loop. C&NW's line here is continually bustling with activity. *Chris Burritt*

A mixture of the old and new C&NW heralds brings us to the realization that railroads, too, are constantly changing. In 1886, the C&NW offered passenger service between Chicago and the Twin Cities in 12½ hours; think, too, of all the fine NorthWestern trains that the road used to sponsor: the *Overland Limited, China and Japan Fast Mail, Los Angeles Limited* and the *North Coast Limited.* Opening of Proviso Yard—largest freight yard in the U.S. at the time—took place in 1929. Now the C&NW is heavy into piggyback and coal traffic. Things change, but we always remember the good old days, especially those of the C&NW. *Charles Zeiler*

Chicago, Burlington & Quincy

It appeared more powerful than the 900-hp it packed, but the #9900 EMC *Pioneer Zephyr,* built in 1934 for the Burlington, raised a lot of eyebrows. More than 2 million people saw it during a 222-city, 30,437-mile exhibition, when it was new. Here, the articulated train passes through Lincoln, Nebraska, on one of its many runs. Today #9900 is on display at the Museum of Science & Industry in Chicago. This Zephyr was the first diesel-powered passenger train in the country. *Charles Zeiler*

ABOVE. March 11, 1965 was a cold day on the "Q" as a pair of E units bring their commuter trains to a stop at Naperville, Illinois. The stop will be brief, and then the conductor will give the highball and off they'll scramble again. The commuter line ran west 38 miles out to Aurora. *Charles Zeiler*

The observation-dome *Silver Chateau* #235 was built by Budd and is seen here bringing up the rear of the famous *Denver Zephyr* that ran between Chicago, Denver and Colorado Springs. Leaving Chicago at the stroke of 5 in the evening, Denver would be in sight by 8:30 the next morning. By 10:40 a.m., you would be in C. Springs, compliments of the Rio Grande. *Charles Zeiler*

"Everywhere West" was the Burlington's famous slogan, and truthfully, Burlington could deliver passengers to such places as Omaha, Kansas City, Denver, Salt Lake City, Los Angeles and San Francisco—12,000 miles of track in 14 states in 1930. Name trains included the *Fast Mail, Denver Limited, Aristocrat* and *Ak-Sar-Ben.* The *Ak-Sar-Ben* and the *Blackhawk* had valet service, terminal telephones and a mid-train salon club car divided between lounging space and single rooms with *real beds.* The *Aleutian* was probably once part of that passenger train era, but shown here years later amongst its streamlined brethren. *Chris Burritt*

With Chicago as its backdrop, the Burlington sends out another commuter train headed by #9943. The date is October of 1962, and the weather is about to get a lot worse, making Chicago's nickname Windy City a reality. *Jerry Carson*

Burlington motive power was always *first class* and always in evolution. C.H. Murphy in David Morgan's book *Diesels West!* said it best: "Progress is a continuous, never-ending process." Witness here then the evolution: #9981A, a 2,400-hp E9; behind it, an E5 B unit, and behind it, the articulated *Nebraska Zephyr. Chris Burritt*

PRECEDING PAGE, TOP. ''Q'' #9153 SW6 pushes two side dump cars around the Aurora railroad shops on July 17, 1965. BOTTOM. One of the Burlington's local passenger trains in 1965. *Both photos, Chris Burritt*

RIGHT. Motorcar #9767 takes up where other passenger trains left off at St. Joseph, Missouri on February 15, 1958. The RPO-baggage, made by EMC-Pullman in 1930, was scrapped three years later. *Jerry Carson*

BELOW. It's early afternoon in November of 1971 at Highlands, Illinois west of Chicago. Note the second unit's unusual paint scheme with green nose. *Bill Raia*

The time: 3:00 p.m. *The place:* Chicago's Union Station. *The railroad:* Burlington. *The train: The Afternoon Zephyr. The route:* Chicago to Minneapolis-St. Paul, arriving in St. Paul at 9:45 p.m. and in Minneapolis at Great Northern's station 35 minutes later. *The equipment:* vista-dome parlor cars, dining-refreshment car and vista-dome reclining seat chair cars. *The cost:* $15.70 first class to Minneapolis, or $28.30 roundtrip. *The photographer: Chris Burritt*

The westbound *Empire Builder*—a combined Burlington and Great Northern streamliner—hugs the banks of the Mississippi River at Savannah, Illinois on its daily trip from Chicago to Portland, Oregon. The great dome train featured tape recorded music, radio reception and coach porter service, not to mention the dome full-length lounge, the Pullman sleeping cars, a dining car, a ''ranch'' lounge for meals and beverages between Chicago and Seattle and reclining seat chair cars. *Chris Burritt*

Denver's Union Station and the *Denver Zephyr* fit hand-in-glove, as in this '50s scene. What a thrill to step aboard in Chicago at 5 p.m. right before dinner and wake up the following morning with the majestic Rocky Mountains beckoning in the distance. *Collection of Bill Raia*

This E5A was assigned to the Colorado & Southern, to which the Burlington acquired control in 1908. In the shops now, tomorrow this unit could be piloting the daily *Texas Zephyr* between Denver and Houston. *Chris Burritt*

ABOVE. A freight with four F units heads eastbound near Galva, Illinois toward Kewanee in 1965. *Chris Burritt*

RIGHT. Streaking like a bullet (about 90 miles per hour) through Galva, Illinois is one of the "Q's" *Zephyrs* in 1966. *Chris Burritt*

LEFT. Burlington power and Northern Pacific passenger equipment were featured on the *North Coast Limited* from Chicago to St. Paul, Minnesota. From there, NP power took over the longer leg of the trip to Portland, Oregon. *Chris Burritt*

ABOVE. Engine #4960 is a steam locomotive number that conjurs up thrilling moments from the past. Buffs used to ride behind that famous locomotive on Burlington fantrips in the '60s. At Zearing, Illinois and turning around for the trip back home to Chicago, #4960 crosses over the Burlington main line. *Chris Burritt*

An EMD-built Burlington switcher provides color in front of the enginehouse on a bright summer day in western Illinois. *Chris Burritt*

CB&Q/C&S #828 with snowplow attached and wooden caboose trailing is at Climax, Colorado in September of 1971. Note safety stripes on side of diesel. *Jerry Carson*

A C&S wood caboose is a fitting end to this train photographed 25 years ago by Chris Burritt. Today, many of America's freight trains don't even have cabooses.

ABOVE, RIGHT. A like-new 1,750-hp SD9 switches the team track at Galva, Illinois. The unit, part of the series 325-344, was built in 1954 and 10 years ago from the date of this picture. *Chris Burritt*

A Burlington local freight progresses westbound toward Eola, Illinois out of Chicago in 1971. *Bill Raia*

Columbus & Greenville

It all started as the narrow gauge Greenville, Columbus & Birmingham on January 5, 1878. In 1920 the name was changed to the Columbus & Greenville Railroad Co.; three years later the line was sold for $35,000 and renamed *again*. Baldwin-Lima-Hamilton #606 was built in 1951 and here works in the Columbus, Mississippi yards on July 25, 1960. *Richard Wallin*

Denver & Rio Grande Western Standard gauge

One of the long, sleek 6000-series Alco PA diesels of the D&RGW sits in Denver's Union Station in September of 1965 with its passenger train. *Chris Burritt*

An F3A 1,500-hp diesel of 1946 vintage is at Denver Union Station where passengers could board what the Grande called its "See-all Vista-Dome...at SEE-level!" *Chris Burritt*

The 2,000-hp Alco-GE PA-2 #6001 looks flashy in its orange, black and silver apparel. The D&RGW couldn't have chosen a much more brilliant color scheme for its passenger equipment. *Chris Burritt*

A five-unit diesel freight slides through Salida, Colorado, mid-way between Pueblo and Dotsero, on August 25, 1965. Salida was the beginning of the 21.2-mile Monarch branch. *Chris Burritt*

Nos. 135 and 136 SW1200's built in 1965 are seen that same year on D&RGW property; the paint had barely dried when this picture was taken. The units replaced half of the 1941 Alco units on the Rio Grande. *Chris Burritt*

A radio-equipped black cupola caboose with white "flying" Rio Grande lettering rolls through Salida. At left is an old Grande wood box car now used as a storage shed in the railroad yards. *Chris Burritt*

BELOW. An F3 brings its train to a stop and the baggage and mail carts pull up to the headend cars for loading and unloading. Passengers detrain and the engines are refueled if necessary. Crews change, and the conductor waves a highball. The 1,500-hp units are set in motion, and the trip continues over the "Main Line Thru the Rockies" route. *Chris Burritt*

The *Royal Gorge* was a daily train—equipped with chair cars (all seats reserved in advance in the summer), sleeper (10 roomettes, 6 double bedrooms), a Slumbercoach (24 single rooms, 8 double rooms) and a vista-dome-buffet-lounge car (summer season)—from Denver to Salida, passing through, of course, the Gorge and along the Arkansas River. Northbound *Royal Gorge* has Great Northern and Union Pacific cars in the consist this August 20, 1964. *Charles Zeiler*

Three Geeps—with GP-35 #3043 bringing up the rear—plow forward at Salida with a freight to an unknown final destination. *Chris Burritt*

Nine of these 660-hp Baldwin VO660's were on the D&RGW property in 1966; they were built in 1941. The #68 was converted to a booster unit at one point in its life. *Chris Burritt*

This is likely the *Denver Zephyr* operated jointly with the Missouri Pacific between Denver and St. Louis. The Rio Grande picked up the train at Pueblo, and the MoPac operated the 1,021 miles between Pueblo and St. Louis. Thus, this Rio Grande diesel is leading a MoPac diesel unit into Denver's Union Station on August 20, 1964. *Charles Zeiler*

Two workmen check the trucks on a GP7. *Chris Burritt*

An Alco-GE 1,000-hp S2 sits quietly for the camera in September of 1965. *Chris Burritt*

The orange, black and silver caboose is striking, especially when the morning sun hits its side just right. *Chris Burritt*

D&RGW Narrow Gauge

SCENIC LINE OF THE WORLD

Cumbres, the place on the Rio Grande where early railroad crews broke out their "thousand mile lunches," so-called because a man never knew how long the trip over the pass would take in steam days. The soul-satisfying beauty of Cumbres Pass has been widely publicized. Date: July, 1973. *Don Heimburger*

BELOW. K-37's #493 and #494, both rebuilt in 1928 at Burnham Shops from Class C-41 standard gauge 2-8-0s, cross a wide, sky-blue stream on the Alamosa to Chama portion of the D&RGW narrow gauge line in September of 1965. *Chris Burritt*

This old water tank on the narrow gauge portion of the Rio Grande has seen many a battle between man and Nature, especially with the gale force winds, the excessive snow drifts and the frightful thunderstorms that pass through the high Colorado Rockies. *Chris Burritt*

A narrow gauge D&RGW freight moves slowly through the valley as the tracks twist and turn. The first two gondolas are carrying new ties for a track repair project up the line. The crew's waterbag, hanging down from underneath the cab window, is partially visible. *Chris Burritt*

Des Moines & Central Iowa

The Des Moines & Central Iowa, a 25.1-mile line, ran #100, a 600-hp GE 70-tonner. The road was purchased by the C&NW in 1968 and merged into C&NW in 1984. *Charles Zeiler*

Duluth & Northeastern

In August of 1963, the Duluth & Northeastern Railroad at Cloquet, Minnesota was running this 2-8-0 in freight service to Saginaw, 10.19 miles away. Traffic on the shortline includes lumber, pulp, paper and chemicals. Today the line uses EMD SW switchers. In 1964 Potlatch Corp. took control of the line. *Brad Smith*

Duluth, Winnipeg & Pacific

The DW&P today is part of the Canadian National running from Ft. Frances, Ont., to Duluth, Minnesota. This RDC was at Duluth in June of 1958. *Charles Zeiler*

East Branch & Lincoln

The #5 spot on the East Branch & Lincoln at Lincoln, New Hampshire fills the air with smoke in August of 1964. *Photo by L. Gordon Eaton, collection of Brad Smith*

East Troy

ABOVE. The Municipal of East Troy's M-15 (Milwaukee Electric Railway & Light Co.) scampers through East Troy, Wisconsin on June 30, 1966. *Charles Zeiler*

Here the M-15 is getting ready to tow a box car in July of 1965. The line is now a museum railroad open Memorial Day through October. *Brad Smith*

Electro-Motive

#462 was an Electro-Motive demonstrator sandwiched between other units on a Burlington freight train in Cicero, Illinois on April 20, 1965. *Charles Zeiler*

Elgin, Joliet & Eastern

The "J" has direct connections with every railroad entering Chicago, but freight interchanges are made smartly at outlying points away from city congestion. With track mileage at 238, the EJ&E rings the Windy City, only occasionally running through Cook County itself. The line is called "Chicago's Outer Belt." EJ&E SD9 rolls past steel mills at Hammond, Indiana on February 16, 1970. *Owen Leander*

EJ&E's huge, 2,000-hp Baldwin DT 6-6-2000 was a monster no matter how you look at it. The 1948-built locomotive had a number of like kinds on the railroad. *Brad Smith*

#920 approaches Route 34 at Aurora, Illinois on a freight run on July 10, 1965. Aurora is the end of a short branch off the main line of the EJ&E; the line runs south from Porter, Indiana to West Chicago on the west and Waukegan on the north. The line also runs two branches into the South Chicago harbor district from Gary, Indiana. *Charles Zeiler*

Elk River Coal & Lumber

A mountain stream cools the heels of Elk River Coal & Lumber Company #19 three-truck Shay as she makes a crossing without benefit of a ballasted roadbed. The Elk River line was situated in West Virginia when this picture was taken on May 31, 1958. *Jerry Carson*

NEXT PAGE. Erie FA2 #7374 with headlight burning heads up a freight at Hammond, Indiana on July 25, 1965. The locomotive needs a wash, but its beautiful Alco FA style is still refreshing to behold. Note old elevated crossing shanty at left. *Chris Burritt*

Erie-Lackawanna

The Erie Railroad ran from New York in the East to Rochester and Buffalo, on to Youngstown and Cleveland, Cincinnati and a line to Chicago that split at Marion, Ohio. In 1929 the Erie had 2,316 miles of right-of-way and nearly 45,000 cars and 1,100 locomotives. The road went through numerous hard times over the years, including bankruptcy in 1938. The recession of the 1950s prompted it to merge with the Lackawanna in 1960. Engines #850 and #855 escort a train in September of 1960. *Richard Wallin*

An RS3 handles a suburban train with Pullman-green coaches in New Jersey where it ran an extensive commuter service. *Brad Smith*

One of Erie's servicing facilities near Jersey City is busy this fall of 1962 where an Erie PA, an Erie-Lackawanna E unit at right and some switchers are in residence. The E-L merger occurred two years previous in 1960. *Brad Smith*

Already 13 years on the roster, #7094 FA appears not much the worse for wear on the exterior, considering all that has happened to the line since it came aboard in 1949. By 1959 the Erie was down to only 484 locomotives. *Brad Smith*

Sitting like giant monuments to the Golden Days of Railroading, two huge gray concrete coaling towers loom above the Erie tracks in 1962. *Brad Smith*

An S1 switcher of modest means (660-hp) and a bright, apparently new E-L cherry-red caboose saunter up the track in spring of 1965 at Hammond, Indiana. *Chris Burritt*

An E-L PA2 looks sharp in the gray, maroon and yellow dressing awarded her when the two roads merged in 1960. *Brad Smith*

A rugged-looking 1,000-hp S2 awaits assignment at Hammond, Indiana on *"The Friendly Service Route"* in 1965. Still operating over the Erie then were the passenger trains *Phoebe Snow*, *The World's Fair*, *The Twilight* and mail trains *Pacific Express*, *New York Mail* and *The Owl.* The mail trains ran coaches, and snack service was available in the restaurant at Binghamton, New York. *Chris Burritt*

ABOVE. Two freshly painted Geep 9's hustle down the track at Erie-Lackawanna's yard at Hammond, Indiana in the summer of 1965. *Chris Burritt*

LEFT. A 1947-built F3 A unit presents a pretty picture at 47th Street in Chicago on October 31, 1965. *Charles Zeiler*

Florida East Coast

ABOVE. White flags waving in the sultry Florida air, BL2 #601, a 1,500-hp unit, rumbles past the palm-lined tracks at Daytona Beach in September of 1965. *Richard Wallin*

RIGHT. An extremely colorful red-and-yellow GP7 on the Florida East Coast handles a freight through a crossing at Ft. Lauderdale on August 25, 1959. The FEC—The "Speedway to Sunshine" route—ran 764.76 miles from Jacksonville to Miami (with steamship connections to Nassau) and to Key West (with connections to Havana). This was Henry M. Flagler's road. *Collection of Don Heimburger*

An E9 handles train #2 at Daytona Beach on the FEC in August of 1966. *Collection of Don Heimburger*

LEFT. Diesel #652 does some local switching among the palm trees at Daytona Beach in 1966. The FEC was unequivocally the foremost developer of the east coast of Florida. Flagler, a creative man, built or bought what was or would be the finest hotels along the line to attract more people to Florida, people who would arrive by his railroad. Passenger trains on the FEC included the *Miamian, Champion, Dixie Flagler* and the *Havana Special. Collection of Don Heimburger*

Georgia

The 323-mile Georgia Railroad with headquarters at Atlanta ran passenger service between Augusta and Atlanta with two roundtrips daily. Train Nos. 1 and 3 were westbound leaving Augusta daily at 11:45 and 2:20 a.m. respectively, arriving in Atlanta at 5:05 p.m. and 7 a.m. Trains were air conditioned and featured reclining seats, through sleeper and dining car service to New York (with connections with the Atlantic Coast Line; Richmond, Fredericksburg and Potomac; and Pennsylvania Railroad.) Interestingly, mixed service was also offered between Union and Athens, Barnett and Washington (Georgia) and Camak and Macon. Here at Atlanta on May 4, 1970 is #1004, an FP7 built in 1950 and having seen better days. The Georgia Railroad roster included five FP7's, a long list of GP7's and an F3. *Richard Wallin*

Grand Trunk Western

Grand Trunk Western, a Canadian National subsidiary since 1928, with service into the Chicago area, sports the all-American colors of red, white and blue. The GT runs from Chicago on the west to Detroit and Port Huron on the east to Cincinnati on the south. At one time it was controlled by Henry Ford, and was once owned by a Pennsylvania Railroad subsidiary and also the Ann Arbor. In 1982 it placed a bid for the Milwaukee Road which was rejected. The GT's motive power is represented here by #5805, a GP-38 built in 1971 and seen in service at Blue Island, Illinois on May 25, 1974. EMD built a dozen units for GT in the series 5800-5811. *Jerry Carson*

Big #6332 4-8-4 hauls a less than capacity load of one coach on October 29, 1955 at Lansing, Illinois, offering the engine a brief respite from more intensive labors. Behind the GT was the idea to reduce the barriers between the United States and Canada and promote the freer movement of goods across the borders. New England fisherman, farmers and woodsman helped with the "Grand Trunk Dream" and were loyal to the railroad line. The Grand Trunk is named after a famous old highway in British Imperial India. *Jerry Carson*

Engine #4139, a 1,750-hp GP9 originally #4541, was wrecked and then re-numbered to #4139 in 1959. At Royal Oak, Michigan in July of 1970, it is leading a five car suburban train and heading for Pontiac. The red nose of the diesel alerts motorists of an approaching train. *Richard Wallin*

ABOVE. With automobile parts as well as assembled autos probably the bulk of its carloads, #1432 and two other Geeps lead a freight train at Durand, Michigan. The date is April of 1974. *Jerry Carson*

LEFT. One of 15 SW900's owned by the Grand Trunk, #7266 is seen at Milwaukee, out of its own territory. The closest the GT's trackage got to the Beer City was Chicago, although there are any number of reasons this switcher could be in Wisconsin in December of 1964. *Brad Smith*

ABOVE. Lined up at GTW's Elsdon Yard in Chicago on June 13, 1965 are F3 #9011, and GP9's #4557 and #4134. The F3 appears to be on its last legs. *Charles Zeiler* BELOW. A GTW three-unit freight barrels down the main line in November of 1970. *Jerry Carson*

ABOVE. In a classic setting virtually any railfan would naturally find should he visit Durand, Michigan, a freight moves on the wye near the passenger station in September of 1979. At Durand, GT trackage fans out to Chicago, Muskegon, Bay City, Port Huron and Detroit. The road has a major yard at Durand. *Don Heimburger*

RIGHT. With a little over 1,500 track miles, the GT operates 265 locomotives and owns nearly 12,000 freight cars. Much of its mileage is in the state of Michigan, where this photo was taken on September 16, 1970. 1,800-hp GP18 #4703 moves through Greenville, Michigan with one of those 12,000 freight cars directly behind. *Jerry Carson*

Great Northern

Behind Great Northern's famous *Empire Builder,* the *Western Star* loomed as one of the great GN passenger trains. Leaving over CB&Q tracks from Chicago's Union Station at 10:30 a.m. every day, the *Western Star* proceeded to St. Paul, Minnesota, shown here, arriving at 7:15 p.m. From there to Seattle, the train progressed on a fascinating journey through hills and mountains, deep gorges and green forests and past crystal clear lakes and streams. Outside of Everett, Washington the passenger train reached Cascade Tunnel, one of the great engineering projects of all time, piercing the solid granite of the formidable Cascade Range for a distance of 7.79 miles. A huge ventilating system enables diesels to run through the tunnel. The *Star* stopped at Glacier Park and Belton, the eastern and western rail entrances to Glacier National Park. Equipment featured on the *Western Star* included reclining seat coaches, diner-lounge car and 16 duplex roomettes/4 double bedroom sleepers. The train featured radio and coach porter service. In 1966 when this photo was taken, a roundtrip ticket was $126.80 in first class or $99.75 coach class. The western state mountains will be a thrill to see in winter's white as this train, still boarding at the station, moves through Montana, Idaho and Washington. *Charles Zeiler*

With a 2,000-hp E7 by its side, #679 GP9 huddles to keep warm at St. Paul in 1966. *Charles Zeiler*

A GN F unit moves through the turnouts during switching maneuvers at St. Paul. *Charles Zeiler*

Green Bay & Western

ABOVE. Green Bay & Western was originally chartered in 1866 to serve points between Green Bay, Wisconsin and the Mississippi River. The independently-owned line has remained all-Alco since it dieselized. Its 255 miles now extend all the way east to Kewaunee where lake ferries used to provide frequent service from Michigan points such as Ludington and Frankfort. GBW #309 is an RS11 built in 1956. Its bright red paint shows up clearly here at Kewaunee. *Brad Smith*

RIGHT. Wearing a new coat of red and gray color, complete with gray trucks, GB&W #305, an RS20, rebuilt by the railroad with a 2,000-hp engine, sifts through freight cars at Wisconsin Rapids, Wisconsin, about midway between each end point of the line. *Richard Wallin*

Gulf, Mobile & Ohio

The Gulf, Mobile & Ohio today still fascinates many historians and railfans. The GM&O's southern hospitality and its scrappy underdog image, combined with its flair for upbeat paint schemes and service-oriented passenger trains, made it a standout. #102 E unit sits waiting at Chicago. *Chris Burritt*

ABOVE. The twin cities of Bloomington-Normal, Illinois was the home of a huge railroad yard for the GM&O. Formed in 1938 to combine the Mobile & Ohio and the Gulf, Mobile & Northern, the line extended from Chicago to New Orleans, after it merged with the Alton Railroad in 1947. Engine #100 passes through Bloomington. *Chris Burritt*

RIGHT. GM&O operated a Chicago to Joliet (37.2 miles) commuter train, here seen coming out of the Loop. *Charles Zeiler*

An RS1 crosses a neighbor's railroad tracks in Joliet, Illinois on June 7, 1972. Can't miss those numbers on the cab! *Rail Photos Unlimited*

A small 660-hp SW1 in red and silver markings switches GM&O freight on "The Rebel Route." *Collection of Don Heimburger*

NEXT PAGE. An oversize load gets special attention and care by the crew and an RS2 and caboose, apparently waiting on a siding here for another train to pass. *Collection of Don Heimburger*

ABOVE. Two 1,500-hp FA1's deliver supplies to a construction site on the GM&O in 1965. *Collection of Don Heimburger*

RIGHT. An EMD test unit visits the GM&O in April of 1964. *Collection of Don Heimburger*

PREVIOUS PAGE. It must be show-and-tell time on the GM&O by their publicity director's decision to show this brand spanking-new SD40 delivered from EMD in March of 1966. A dozen were built for the GM&O in the same grouping. *Collection of Don Heimburger*

An F3 is in Bloomington, its underbody covered with "road dirt." The date is August 17, 1972. *Rail Photos Unlimited*

Venice, Illinois is the location of this GM&O scene where two GP35's sit out against a darkening, rain-filled sky in June of 1975. *Jerry Carson*

BELOW. Locomotives #101 and 101A with a passenger train back into St. Louis Union Station in 1970. This is likely *The Limited,* the Chicago to St. Louis passenger train arriving in late afternoon. *Jerry Carson* NEXT PAGE. #805B leads a three-unit diesel freight through Bloomington in August of 1966. *Chris Burritt*

Hutchinson & Northern

One of the very first railroads to be listed in the May, 1965 *Official Guide* was the Hutchinson & Northern Railway, a 6-mile line extending from Hutchinson to Carey Lake and Carey Mine, Kansas. At Hutchinson, it connected with the Santa Fe, Rock Island and MoPac. It operated for freight service only. *Chris Burritt*

Hoosac Tunnel & Wilmington

This solid little 380-hp GE 44-tonner originally was, surprisingly, D&RGW #39, then S&E #14 before arriving on the HT&W. The 11-mile HT&W is a Hoosac Tunnel, Mass. to Readsboro, Vermont line. *Brad Smith*

Illinois Terminal

The Illinois Terminal started as a streetcar line serving Champaign and Urbana, Illinois in 1890. Seventy-five years later two IT SW1200's grapple with a freight drag west of Decatur, Illinois. *Photo by Lou Schmitz, collection of Charles Zeiler*

Three IT diesels roll down the track near East Peoria, Illinois at Farmdale Junction on September 16, 1979. By 1980, the IT had trimmed its operation to two-thirds trackage rights on existing railroads and one-third owned. In 1981 the N&W purchased the line, and it was completely gone as an entity in May of 1982. *Bob Nicholson*

Illinois Central

The famous Illinois Central Railroad began in 1851 as a line between Cairo to Galena, Illinois and a line between Centralia and Chicago. The IC benefitted as the first railroad to be given land grant status by President Millard Fillmore in 1850. The IC was the major north-south railroad in the country, although at times management would liked to have been an east-west railroad instead. The IC was especially known for its fine passenger trains such as the *Panama Limited, City of New Orleans* and the *City of Miami.* Paducah, Kentucky was where IC steam power was rebuilt and maintained. In 1972, the IC merged with the GM&O to form Illinois Central Gulf. On May 13, 1967, 2,400-hp E9 #4035 sits at the sanding tower in Chicago. *Owen Leander*

An inbound *Panama Limited* passes another outbound passenger train at 115th Street (Kensington) on IC's hot main line in south Chicago in July of 1965. This stretch of right-of-way saw a profuse number of trains daily. *Chris Burritt*

Three of IC's black Geeps with the green diamond under the cab windows hustle a freight through Central Illinois in mid-1966. In 1929, the IC system boasted 1,762 locomotives, but that had dropped to 766 by 1971. Fans could watch IC's passenger trains barreling down the Illinois corridor as fast as 100 miles an hour in pre-Amtrak days. *Charles Zeiler*

E7 #4016 and sister unit hover around IC's 12th Street Station in May of 1965, probably awaiting assignment to one of several trains: *Southern Express, The Louisiana, The Seminole,* the *Panama Limited, The Creole* or one of the *City* trains. Roundtrip between Chicago and New Orleans cost only $52.00 in 1965. *Brad Smith*

An IC GP7 at right does switching while a yard supervisor checks out a load of automobiles at left in Markham Yard. The IC ran dispatch freight trains with initials of towns as the symbols for trains, such as NC-6 for New Orleans to Chicago. *Collection of Don Heimburger*

NEXT PAGE. Amidst the jungle of overhead wires, turnouts and signals comes one of IC's electrics into Randolph Street Station, end of the line on IC's commuter division which hauls thousands of commuters to the Loop every day. *Chris Burritt*

Two 3,000-hp GP40's pull a ''public relations'' train of newly-painted 50-foot box cars through the southern Illinois landscape so that IC's photographer can get a good picture for promotion purposes. *Collection of Don Heimburger*

This IC electric car has orange safety paint on its end, perhaps done as a test since this was not standard practice on these cars. This train is at 55th Street in Chicago in June of 1978. *Charles Zeiler*

A 2,250-hp E8 still has water dripping down its side after being washed on IC property in Chicago. *Brad Smith*

In 1965 the IC was cooperating with the New York Central on the daily train *The James Whitcomb Riley* from IC's Central Station to Cincinnati and beyond over C&O rails to Norfolk, Virginia. The *Riley* was an all-coach seats reserved train. *Chris Burritt*

Streamliners, electric commuter trains, long freights, transfer freights and freight locals were all run on IC trackage south of Central Station. Here a local is at Keningston. *Chris Burritt*

Illinois Midland

Illinois Midland 0-4-0 #4 pulled freight for this short line that last ran steam in 1958 around Millington, Illinois (population: 400). The line branched off to a grain elevator from the Burlington main. *Collection of Bill Raia*

Indiana Harbor Belt

An NW2 and an SW9 together bring 2,200-hp to an IHB train at Hammond, Indiana on July 25, 1965. *Chris Burritt*

Kansas City Terminal

The eight locomotives owned by Kansas City Terminal include #75, an EMD SW1200, seen switching the passenger terminal in 1965. The line is owned by 10 other roads. *Chris Burritt*

A KCT switcher pulls a Wabash combine into position for another run of the Wabash Domeliner *City of St. Louis* or possibly the *City of Kansas City* trains between St. Louis and Kansas City in 1965 at the Kansas City passenger terminal. *Chris Burritt*

#71 of the KCT was built in 1964, relatively late. The safety end stripes and the diamond insignia look sharp. *Chris Burritt*

Kansas City Southern

ABOVE. This 1952-built E8 is at the Kansas City passenger terminal backing down the track into the train shed to hook up with its consist, perhaps the *Southern Belle* or passenger train No. 15-9. *Richard Wallin* BELOW. KCS Baldwin S12 draws a transfer run. *Chris Burritt*

Keokuk Junction

Not-hard-to-see Alco S2 is on the 4.5-mile Keokuk Junction Railway at Keokuk, Iowa in 1982. The previous year the line was initiated by acquiring trackage from the former Rock Island. *Bob Nicholson*

LaSalle & Bureau County

The LaSalle & Bureau County operated for a total of 15 miles between LaSalle, Illinois, Midway, Hegeler, LaSalle Jct. and Ladd. Their #6 is a Baldwin V0660 built in 1946. *Chris Burritt*

Livonia, Avon & Lakeville

The LA&L was formed in 1964 to operate an 8.5-mile ex-Erie line from Avon to Lakeville, New York. For a while the road ran excursion service. RS1 #20 is a colorful Alco product. *Rail Photos Unlimited*

Louisville & Nashville

This Louisville & Nashville *Humming Bird* coach was spotted on the Cincinnati Union Terminal Railroad on January 24, 1959. "The Old Reliable" was the name given to the proud L&N Railroad which also ran the famed *Pan-American* passenger train. *Collection of Don Heimburger*

ABOVE. A 1,500-hp FA1 and sisters in alternating black and white stripes and yellow lettering appear impassive at East St. Louis on December 7, 1963. *Richard Wallin* RIGHT. A five-unit freight led by a 2,800-hp U28B is ready to leave Corbin, Kentucky in 1972. *Brad Smith*

An L&N FA2 that's already nine years old looks none the worse for wear in this June 1965 photo at Radnor, Tennessee. *Richard Wallin*

"The Old Reliable" was a signature on these two-bay tuscan red hoppers that carried the livelihood of the L&N—coal. The time is long ago—April of 1958, and just seeing this peaked-end hopper brings back railroad memories of the past. *Collection of Don Heimburger*

NEXT PAGE. A five-unit Maine Central freight cuts through the thick pine scent and mist at Willey House, Crawford Notch, New Hampshire in July of 1964. You can't help but notice the front of this F7. *Brad Smith*

Maine Central

The headlight ablaze like a white flare, Maine Central F3 awaits a green board before proceeding at Crawford Notch. *Brad Smith*

Manufacturer's Junction

Cicero, Illinois is the home of the Manufacturer's Junction Railway, owned by AT&T Technologies, Inc. Owning about 25 freight cars and two locomotives, both SW1's, the line operates a total of 10½ miles, mostly used for switching. Here in 1966, #7 is handsomely decked out. *Charles Zeiler*

Manufacturers Railway

The Manufacturers Railway consists of 42 miles of trackage between St. Louis, Missouri and East St. Louis, Illinois. Its 10 locomotives are Alco S2s and an S4, and some EMD switchers. These switchers haul freight over the MoPac Yard in St. Louis. *Jerry Carson*

Missouri Pacific

Engines #946 and #944—two Alco RS11's—are road switchers pulling a long string of reefers through the Gateway City, St. Louis, in September of 1972. *Jerry Carson*

Bringing in one of MoPac's passenger trains to the Kansas City Union Station is 2,000-hp E7 #24 followed by a set of headend cars including a tuscan red box car and express cars. The *Eagle* passenger trains on this route (St. Louis-Kansas City-Omaha) included diner-parlor cars, dome-coach, grill-coach and sleepers. *Chris Burritt*

A diner car off one of the Missouri Pacific *Eagles* gets a shove from a Kansas City Terminal switcher in the process of making up a passenger train. Lunch anyone? *Chris Burritt*

A GP7 #214 (note hastily-painted number under cab window) switches some freight in September of 1965. The Missouri Pacific *Railway* was organized in 1876—about 100 years before this photo was taken—and was a sprawling road that stretched from Chicago to Pueblo, Colorado to Brownsville, Texas, New Orleans and Memphis. It basically engulfed the states of Kansas, Texas, Louisiana, Arkansas and Missouri. *Chris Burritt*

A MoPac switcher escorts a line of freight cars through Sauget, Illinois in March of 1973. Before the MoPac merged with the Union Pacific and Western Pacific, it operated 11,500 miles of trackage. *Jerry Carson*

Of the number series #38-41, this is an E8. The last of the E units on MoPac were #7018-7021 (later renumbered to #38-41) and delivered in June of 1950. B units were not purchased at this time, but the new A units were used with already existing combinations of A and B units. By the mid-60s most of the E's were scrapped. *Chris Burritt*

NEXT PAGE. F7A on the Missouri-Kansas-Texas (KATY) was one of other F7's replaced by more powerful, newer units such as the GP38-2's and the GP40's. Sold to Precision Engineering in 1971, they finished their days working for the Chicago & NorthWestern Railroad. *Chris Burritt*

126

ABOVE. 1,200-hp S12 #37 is part of Katy's first-generation diesels; a total of 15 of these were purchased in 1951 and 1952. *Chris Burritt*

LEFT. Locomotive switchers #8 and #17 work nose to nose pooling their combined 2,200-hp. The #8 is an NW2 and the #17 is an SW9. *Chris Burritt*

All the AS16's on the KATY were delivered in the early '50s and were repowered between the years 1958-60 by EMD except for one unit. The KATY runs from Omaha-Council Bluffs on the north to San Antonio and Galveston on the south. Mileage: 2,175. *Chris Burritt*

ABOVE. A bright red FP7 #79A with an FA diesel directly behind is at Parsons, Kansas in this 1968 photo. The simple, uncluttered paint scheme was still attractive. *Rail Photos Unlimited*

LEFT. SW9 #18 is beginning to lose some of its paint but remains comely. *Chris Burritt*

Monon

MONON RAILROAD
AND CONNECTIONS

LEFT AND BELOW. Packing 2,750-hp, this DL628 is part of Alco's Century series featuring six axles for better tractive effort. There were 181 of these 69-foot-long units built. The Monon's C-628's were equipped with dual controls, and their stay on the Monon was short-lived, being sold to the Lehigh Valley. The units were replaced by four-axle C-420's which didn't wear Monon's track so heavily. Note the classification lights above the numberboards—red on the inside, green in the middle and white on the outside. *Both photos, Chris Burritt*

Monon NW-2 #14 at Hammond, Indiana pulls one of its own 40-foot box cars and others in the yards. The Monon, officially named the Chicago, Indianapolis & Louisville, filed for bankruptcy in 1933, but it continued to operate even though business was not adequate on the line. The L&N merged with the Monon in 1971. *Chris Burritt*

New Orleans Trolley

New Orleans beckons visitors from all over the world for many reasons—the mighty Mississippi, Bourbon Street and Jackson Square, the jazz and nightlife, the history and the delicious Cajun food. Then there's the green and red trolley cars that run along St. Charles Avenue and through the downtown shopping district. The cars are original, run frequently, and rides are inexpensively priced. On St. Charles Avenue, the trolleys travel down the middle of the parkway. The line is operated by the Regional Transit Authority. It's a convenient and low-cost way to travel. Date: April, 1967. *Chris Burritt*

New York Central

New York Central's steam locomotives could be classed as "functional requisites"—only what was needed was put on them, what wasn't needed was left off. This 2-8-2 at Kankakee, Illinois in November of 1955 is no exception. *Jerry Carson*

Diesel power consisting of only one Geep evidently is enough to haul this long freight at East St. Louis, Illinois in 1971. *Jerry Carson*

ABOVE. "Sharknose" #3807 was a 1,600-hp RF-16 built by Baldwin in December 1951. Sixteen years later, after working a majority of the time on the Big Four (Cleveland, Cincinnati, Chicago & St. Louis), the unit was sold to GE. Other units shown here are #3703 and #3806. The units are parked at the Rock Island terminal in Council Bluffs, Iowa on July 9, 1958. *Richard Wallin*

LEFT. An RS3 with the NYC lightning stripes gets a spin on the turntable at Beacon Park, Massachusetts in April of 1963. *Brad Smith*

ABOVE. A four-unit NYC diesel freight rides high over the water in this picturesque scene along the "Water Level Route." *Brad Smith*

RIGHT. A brace of Budd-built railcars charge up the line on the New York Central. Almost 20 of these were built by Budd for the NYC in the early '50s. Nearly all were later sold to the Penn Central. *Brad Smith*

ABOVE. A trio of FA's park at rest until their next assignment is announced. The front unit appears to have been splattered with water recently. *Brad Smith*

LEFT. #8213, an RS2 and an F unit are waking up to a bright 1962 day in West Detroit, Michigan. *Jerry Carson*

Obviously a mail train, it's one of those unusual trains that is fun to remember seeing. Mail trains are mostly a thing of the past. It's September of 1962. *Brad Smith*

Bright yellow summer flowers in full bloom seem to contradict the sad status of the black and white Fairbanks-Morse 2,000-hp H20-44's on the rip track at East End Yard at the Illinois-Indiana border. Like the coaling tower behind them, these hefty 51-foot-long 1949 units will be retired soon. Less than a year later, Nos. 7112, 7118 and 7113 were sold for scrap. Originally the units were purchased from the Indiana Harbor Belt in 1950. *Chris Burritt*

ABOVE. Barking out loud, crisp commands as she prances down the track is 4-8-2 Mohawk #3024, a dual-purpose L-4a. The Mohawks featured the largest tenders on the NYC, consisting of 43 tons capacity. They were capable of hauling a very heavy freight train, followed immediately by a trip pulling one of the NYC's passenger trains during World War II. The Mohawks were called the backbone of the steam fleet. Date is September 17, 1950. LEFT. Here's #3024 again at West Brookfield, Massachusetts on December 2, 1948. *Both photos by Lawson Hill, collection of Dick Bowers*

ABOVE. NYC #102 electric stands at Mott Haven, Bronx, New York in 1962 awaiting marching orders which could come at any moment. *Jerry Carson*

RIGHT. This could be any number of NYC daily "Water Level Route" passenger trains that plied the rails between Chicago's LaSalle Street Station and Boston and New York in the mid-60s. On October 3, 1965, #4011 E7 with the familiar "cigar band" around its waist pulls out for another run. *Charles Zeiler*

New Haven

ABOVE. A New Haven steam special at Putnam, Connecticut on July 19, 1953 trots past the station with white flags waving. *Brad Smith*

LEFT. The New Haven Dover Street yards in Boston shows the early '60s NH power; from left, Budd rail car, Alco-GE FA1 and Alco-GE PA2. *Brad Smith*

A 1,750-hp EMD FL9 rushes by a highway crossing in an attempt to remain "on the advertised" in June of 1962. *Brad Smith*

Train #508, a daily except Sundays and holidays, is at East Greenwich, Rhode Island in September of 1965. The #508 was a Providence to Boston passenger local, leaving at 8:47 a.m. and arriving in Boston at South Station at 9:50. The 44 miles and eight station stops were covered in 1 hour and 3 minutes. *Brad Smith*

ABOVE. An FM H16-44, surrounded by brethern locomotives, sits at Cedar Hill Yard in New Haven, Connecticut. The FA's on adjacent tracks are definitely in need of a coat of new paint. *Brad Smith*

LEFT. Through the years the New Haven had survived reorganization, business recessions and trucking competition. The road was known for heavy-duty main line railroading and has been a favorite of fans for many years. On the last day of 1968, Penn Central purchased the NH. Four years earlier, #0988 looks quite cheerful. *Brad Smith*

ABOVE. Train #525, pulled by RS3 #526 makes its 2:14 p.m. Saturday only stop at East Greenwich, R.I. The train ran from Boston to New London. *Brad Smith*

RIGHT. In charge of a New Haven passenger train, FL9 #2012 passes another passenger train at Attleboro, Massachusetts where a branch of the NH split off to Taunton. *Brad Smith*

Highballing it with a freight drag over the Thames River at New London, Connecticut in July of 1962 is FA1 #0416. *Brad Smith*

LEFT. With tractive effort of 99,420 pounds each, a trio of 3,300-hp GE electrics pause at New Haven, Connecticut looking as nice as the day they were delivered. *Brad Smith*

NEXT PAGE. Norwich, where this scene was shot, is on the Groton to Worcester line of the New Haven. *Brad Smith*

A four-unit diesel freight with two RS units in the front comes charging down the high iron on a beautiful spring day in 1962. *Brad Smith*

An Alco HH660 with local freight rumbles through Quidnick, R.I. on freight-only trackage. *Brad Smith*

ABOVE. An H16-44 and its train moves through a snowstorm at East Greenwich, R.I. during the first month of 1964. Almost four years later the NH will cease to exist. *Brad Smith*

A black and yellow F is spliced between two FA1's as a freight rolls over NH rails at Providence, R.I. *Brad Smith*

A NH 1949-built 2,000-hp PA2, complete with proud engineer, get their picture taken in this 1963 scene. *Brad Smith*

A Fairbanks-Morse 1,600-hp diesel pulls a load of freight cars through a cut in April before the greenery has had a chance to show itself. *Brad Smith*

Nickel Plate Road

ABOVE. We're east of Hessville, Indiana in March of 1958. Between 1956 and the recession year of 1958, coal tonnage on the NKP plummeted from 18.3 to 11.1 million tons. By the next year, 1959, passenger revenues hit a post-war high of $3.4 million. The diesel-versus-steam ratio was turning in favor of the diesel. A year earlier 36 more of the growlers were added to the roster. *Jerry Carson*

LEFT. NKP #769, a 2-8-4, proves its worth at Hessville, Indiana on November 14, 1957. This was one of the last strongholds of steam power in the U.S. *Jerry Carson*

ABOVE. When the Nickel Plate first reached Cleveland, it had to purchase two tiny suburban rail lines—the Rocky River Rail Road and the Cleveland, Painesville & Ashtabula in 1881. In 1965, an RS11 and two helper Geeps roll freight tonnage through a much different Cleveland. *Brad Smith*

RIGHT. A 700-class Berkshire—the Nickel Plate was known for its 112 husky Berkshires—rides across the Ohio landscape in full glory—and steam. The #740 was the last active steamer on the NKP west of Bellevue, Ohio. It was sold for scrap in August 1963. Here she's at Fostoria on June 9, 1957. *Jerry Carson*

Geep NKP #485 switches cars on the south side of Chicago in 1966. The NKP entered Chicago through northeastern Indiana and was the westbound point on the Chicago to Buffalo main line. *Chris Burritt*

A reefer block train heads through Hessville, Indiana in 1957. A year earlier NKP Chairman Lynne White said, "Unless a more efficient type of power is developed...operations will be completely dieselized by 1962." But here, right now, coming down the track is #754, and nothing looked so good as steam on the NKP! *Jerry Carson*

Berkshire #765 is two miles west of Sheldon, Illinois on an excursion over the Toledo, Peoria & Western in May of 1980. *Bob Nicholson*

Clipping along at a good pace is NKP #765 on the same fantrip as above. #765 was of the S-2 Class, built by Lima in September of 1944. And what a dynamic rail roadster it was...just feel the power! Bob Nicholson is lineside to record the scene at Canton, Illinois.

Norfolk & Western

ABOVE. Norfolk & Western #600, a J Class 4-8-4, is pulling *The Powhatan Arrow* on a run in August of 1956 at Norwood, Ohio. The 600's were superior in every way, and the machines often went from monthly inspection to monthly inspection without missing a trip. *Collection of Don Heimburger*

Big 4-8-2 #112 was built in 1916-17 by N&W's Roanoke Shops. The #112 had Baker valve gear, a type A superheater, Worthington 4BL feedwater heater and a tender with a capacity of 26 tons of coal and 18,000 gallons of water. Date: July 15, 1956. *Collection of Don Heimburger*

GP9 #783 is at Clare Yard in Cincinnati, Ohio on June 15, 1976. Twenty one years earlier, N&W had made the decision to dieselize and was one of the last major roads to do so because of the vast amounts of on-line coal reserves. *Collection of Don Heimburger*

This classic scene typifies the steam-to-diesel transition that was going on at the N&W in 1958: a Y6a 2-8-8-2 slugs it out at Blue Ridge, Virginia with a two-unit diesel passenger train. *Jerry Carson*

One of the Norfolk, Virginia to Cincinnati Norfolk & Western daily trains—the *Powhatan Arrow* or the *Pocahontas*—takes pause at Suffolk, Virginia in 1966 before moving on. Two Geeps are assigned to the train this day, and the passenger station doesn't appear to be doing a land office business. *Brad Smith*

N&W #1215, a 2-6-6-2 Roanoke-built Class A with a length over couplers of an astonishingly long 121' 10" is masterfully handling her freight assignment at Blue Ridge, Virginia August 14, 1958. *Jerry Carson*

ABOVE. From 1951 to 1953, the N&W built 45 new switchers, 15 each year. The engines were numbered 200 through 244 and designated Class S1a. #232 is at Cleveland, Ohio on July 15, 1956 ready for shipment to Portsmouth, Ohio following arrival of the diesels. This locomotive was being retired. *Collection of Don Heimburger*

LEFT. At Pullman Junction, Illinois in April of 1965, N&W waycar leads train with engine pushing. *Charles Zeiler*

Norfolk Southern

Norfolk Southern #14, a GP18, takes a 30 car train (minus caboose) down former interurban spur trackage at Virginia City in 1974. *Collection of Don Heimburger*

Northern Pacific

Northern Pacific coach, marked with modifications through the years, stands at St. Paul's coach yards circa 1965. *Chris Burritt*

The Chicago to Seattle *Mainstreeter*, with the 427-mile Chicago to St. Paul leg provided courtesy of the CB&Q, departs St. Paul on February 5, 1966. Equipment on Train #1 included Slumbercoaches, a diner-lounge (table d'hote dinners, $3.90) and reclining seat coaches. Slumbercoaches accommodated 40 passengers in 24 single and 8 double rooms. A trip on the *Main Street of the Northwest* was inviting. *Charles Zeiler*

Northwestern Steel and Wire

PRECEDING PAGE. Northwestern Steel and Wire Company in Sterling, Illinois was one of the absolute last strongholds of steam operated by a private firm in the U.S. #28 0-8-0 lets us know she's there! *Brad Smith*

ABOVE. The unofficial slogan of the company was, "A steam locomotive in every box of nails." At one time Northwestern Steel melted down Burlington steamers and made them into nails. *Chris Burritt*

ABOVE. Northwestern Steel used several steamers for shunting cars around the vast plant property, and always had several steamers in reserve, often used for parts. #10 brings out a load of steel wire on flatcars in February of 1974. Best spot to watch the steamers do their duty, without being requested to leave, was on an overhead public vehicular bridge that spanned the plant. *Brad Smith*

LEFT. The 0-8-0's worked day in and day out, and could be seen and heard virtually anywhere on plant property. Railfans delighted in locating the steamers and bringing back rolls of color and black and white film dedicated to the scrappy black switchers. *Chris Burritt*

PAT (Port Authority Transit)

Photographer Charles Zeiler was on this Illini Railroad Club fantrip to inspect Pittsburgh's street railway facilities on February 26, 1966. The old time trolley, on the Port Authority Transit line of Alleghany County, was converted to a work car, hence the "M" designation as part of the number. The trolley was accompanied on the fan excursion by a PCC car, seen down the line. The railfans left from Chicago over the Baltimore & Ohio and are seen here at Winhurst Street in Pittsburgh. *Charles Zeiler*

Pennsylvania

#9089 FM H-10-44, a 1,000-hp diesel, sits at the Whiting, Indiana yards with a Pennsylvania 50-ft box car directly behind in July of 1965. These diesel units were manufactured between 1948 and 1949. *Chris Burritt*

Six freight cars and a caboose is all this mighty Pennsylvania 2-10-4 has attached to its coupler, but heavy tonnage is not refused by this Class J1a. All the J's were built at Pennsy's Altoona Shops between 1942 and 1944 (thus their nickname War Babies). The J's design was borrowed from the C&O. *Jerry Carson*

RIGHT. Only one 2,000-hp E7 is required to draw these few heavy-weights down the track. June of 1962 finds Pennsylvania still serving the nation. *Jerry Carson*

ABOVE. A beefy 2,000-hp Fairbanks-Morse H-20-44 with radio antenna at right and #8713, a 1,200-hp H-12-44 built in 1952 with 62,250 pounds of tractive effort, sit near the sanding tower. The proud Pennsy emblem on #8923 still is there. *Chris Burritt*

LEFT. Elizabeth, New Jersey in 1963 sees an electrified Pennsylvania commuter train whiz by. *Brad Smith*

ABOVE. #5845, a 2,000-hp E7 was from EMD, and Pennsylvania ordered 1,543 diesels from this builder, compared with far fewer from any other builder. This E7 has no doubt seen plenty of passenger action, perhaps on the *Manhattan Limited*, the *Golden Triangle*, *The General* or the *Pennsylvania Limited*. The unit is in Pittsburgh in 1960. *Jerry Carson*

RIGHT. Three Pennsy diesel A units with #5849 on the point are growling past 47th Street in Chicago in May of 1965. *Charles Zeiler*

A consolidation #9447, like many Pennsy "Consols," could be found nearly anywhere on the system. Their numbers proved they were well regarded by the management, and they were used for general light utility, especially in local freight assignments. At Columbus, Ohio in August of 1957 one pulls a string of crummies. *Jerry Carson*

BELOW. A Pennsy GG1 electric on assignment. *Brad Smith*

GG1 #4907 in tuscan red handles a passenger train in 1962. The GG1's were bizarre-looking electric creatures that performed well in Pennsy's extremely heavy traffic. *Brad Smith*

Switcher #9383, an SW7, sits at Whiting, Indiana on July 25, 1965. When Pennsy finally dieselized, it purchased units from every manufacturer. During the war years, Pennsy's freight traffic doubled. *Chris Burritt*

In 1928 artist Grif Teller painted Pennsy's calendar with the steam-powered *Broadway Limited* as the highlight. That was only three years after the Pennsy started commissioning large scale paintings for yearly calendars, and in 1925 and 1926 the same painting was used. That's how important the *Broadway Limited* was to the railroad—and how well regarded this train was by travelers. *The Broadway Limited Operating Through the Steel District* was the 1927 picture caption, and in 1928 Pennsy *again* featured the train, this time with a painting entitled *When The Broadway Meets the Dawn.* Here, Pennsy's pride, the *Broadway Limited,* is at Chicago's Union Station on February 27, 1966 with the observation car *Mt. View* on the rear. *Mt. View* was especially made for the *Broadway.* It contained two master bedrooms, another bedroom and a buffet lounge. The very rear lounge compartment seated up to 10, with 15 more in the forward lounge. Between the two lounges was an etched glass partition which provided an open yet divided spaciousness. This group of cars were the only tapered blunt end observation cars ever built. *Charles Zeiler*

Reading

The Reading had a long history of owning and controlling other railroad lines; in fact, that's how it grew. Coal traffic was the key to revenue on the line, supplementing that with bridge traffic. Being an Eastern road, (Atlantic City, Jersey City, Philadelphia, Wilmington, Harrisburg) it also was a passenger-carrying line. Two RDC's come around the curve in this idyllic setting in June of 1969. *Brad Smith*

ABOVE. A brace of Reading RS3's pound down the iron at Saucon Yard, Bethelem, Pennsylvania, end of the branch from Philadelphia. Hauling coal is one of Reading's mainstays, and Reading owned more than 43,000 freight cars in 1929, many of them coal hoppers. *Jerry Carson*

RIGHT. Not a very inspired paint scheme for these Reading RS units, but cost-cutting measures on many American railroads in the '60s and '70s dictated that no stone be left unturned to increase profitability. *Brad Smith*

Soo Line

The Minneapolis, St. Paul & Sault Ste. Marie Railroad, commonly referred to as the Soo Line, was conceived as early as 1883, and construction began the next year at Cameron, Wisconsin, building west to Turtle Lake and east to Bruce, a total of 46 miles. Eighty-one years later, a pair of F7's pull out of the yard at Milwaukee. *Brad Smith*

Two Soo GP35's and a wood caboose move on parallel tracks next to a Chicago & Eastern Illinois freight at 47th Street in Chicago. *Charles Zeiler*

A trio of diesels—#2226B F unit, a U30C and a GP35—is near Minneapolis-St. Paul with a long freight on June 1, 1968. The "U Boats" as they were called were delivered to the railroad in 1968 and ran for 10 years; they had pulling power but didn't fit Soo's power scenario. *Richard Wallin*

Stretching from Sault Ste. Marie on the east to Chicago on the south and Whitetail, Montana on the west, Soo's locomotives roamed the upper Midwest states. #2555 GP9 is at Shoreham Yard roundhouse in Minneapolis on October 3, 1982, perhaps waiting for repairs. *Bob Nicholson*

A former Wisconsin Central F7A and company are at 47th Street Chicago in 1965. *Charles Zeiler*

BELOW. Former Duluth, South Shore & Atlantic Ry. RS1 is 19 years old in this photo. *Brad Smith*

Southern Pacific

This PA3 built in 1953 sits at the Oakland, California sanding towers. This was part of the last order of Alco-GE DP-11's, bringing the total of PA and PB's on the SP to 66. *Brad Smith*

1,600-hp RSD5 at Ogden, Utah on October 3, 1958, five years after it was delivered. The RSD's were used system-wide and some RSD units featured safety-stripe-painted underbody tanks. *Charles Zeiler*

ABOVE. A smattering of SP power appears at San Francisco in 1966, all with the distinct red and gray paint scheme. *Brad Smith*

RIGHT. The SP's interest in the Krauss-Maffei diesels was because of the need for greater horsepower, more tractive effort in the mountains and reduction of power units. The K-M units delivered 4,000-hp. *Jerry Carson*

PRECEDING PAGE. TOP. Fairbanks-Morse H-24-66 Trainmaster and single bi-level commuter coach make time at San Francisco, July of 1968. *Brad Smith* BOTTOM. Various SP diesel paint schemes are displayed in this 1962 scene in California. *Jerry Carson*

ABOVE. "Black widow" paint scheme on F7s at San Francisco's diesel facilities was captured on film by Brad Smith in July of 1968.

LEFT. An Alco S3 shoves cars around at San Francisco getting ready for the next SP passenger train which could be *Sunset Golden State, City of San Francisco, San Francisco Overland* or others. *Brad Smith*

Fairbanks-Morse H12-44, with two old steam locomotive headlights adorning each end, was built in 1952. In 1948 FM loaned the SP a 1,000-hp H10-44 demonstrator for tests and evaluation. When the SP placed an order for these FM units, they had been upgraded to 1,200-hp. *Brad Smith*

Southern

Southern Railway is known for its public relations-minded management. Because people relate more to passenger trains than freight trains, it's logical to sponsor excursions that carry *people.* #610 here—with auxiliary tender—is on a Governor's Special trip near Shelbyville, Kentucky, enroute to the State Fair at Louisville in August of 1979. *Bob Nicholson*

LOOK AHEAD-LOOK SOUTH

Spokane International

One of the Union Pacific-owned railroads is the Spokane International, a 152-mile line extending from Spokane, Washington to Eastport, Idaho. The line runs through the very narrow top finger of Idaho. #1215 is an RS1, and the box car behind it is an old Santa Fe outside-braced type. The freight-only SI serves such towns as East Farms, Corbin Junction, Vay, Samuels, Deep Creek, Bonners Ferry, Meadow Creek and Addie—names that evoke peaceful and serene forests and lakes, small communities where everyone knows everyone else and where the railroad is pretty important. If you didn't see the road name on the side of the diesel, you'd immediately think that you were looking at a Union Pacific locomotive. *Chris Burritt*

Springfield Terminal

The Springfield Terminal Railway is all of 5.41 miles long, extending from Charleston, New Hampshire to Springfield, Vermont. The shortline also does switching on other railroads. This handsomely-painted GE 44-tonner supplies 380-hp and was built in 1941. Today, the line's power is a Geep 7. *Brad Smith*

St. Louis-San Francisco (Frisco)

The later, less fanciful painting scheme of the St. Louis-San Francisco is represented on the first four units. This freight is growling through St. Louis, Missouri on November 21, 1970—23 years after the first road diesels came on Frisco property. In 1948 the first of 36 four-unit EMD F3's arrived, and F7s came on board between March 1949 and February of 1951. *Richard Wallin*

ABOVE. Dolled up after a re-numbering in 1968, F7 #34 (previously #5034) is at Tulsa, Oklahoma. Note the flashing yellow safety light at top center. The F units were purchased by the Frisco to replace steam power, almost with a one for one replacement. *Rail Photos Unlimited*

A Baldwin 1,000-hp VO, delivered in January of 1944 to the Frisco, sits abandoned without an engineer at the throttle. The last Baldwin purchased by the Frisco was in 1948. #200 was the first diesel purchased; it also was a VO-1000. *Chris Burritt*

St. Joseph Terminal

You're looking at exactly half the entire motive power roster of the St. Joseph Terminal Railroad Company located at St. Joseph, Missouri. The 11-mile line was operated for switching purposes only. The SW1 has a sister, #2. *Chris Burritt*

Terminal Railroad

With general offices at Union Station in St. Louis, the Terminal Railroad Association of St. Louis in 1965 handled 65 percent of all St. Louis gateway rail traffic. It had direct connections with 17 trunk lines and three switching lines, as well as barge lines. At Union Station, the line handled passenger traffic as shown here hauling away Missouri Pacific varnish. *Charles Zeiler*

Toledo, Peoria & Western

In 1976, America commemorated the bicentennial, and many railroads joined the celebration by painting a diesel unit in special bicentennial colors: the Toledo, Peoria & Western was no exception. EMD GP-30 #700 is fresh in paint at East Peoria, Illinois in May of 1976. *Bob Nicholson*

GP-35 #901 (later renumbered to ATSF #3462) at Ft. Madison, Iowa in November of 1983. *Bob Nicholson*

NEXT PAGE. Steam engines #X3985 and #X4023 in the roundhouse at Cheyenne, Wyoming in September of 1965. *Chris Burritt*

Union Pacific

ABOVE. One thing you can always count on with Union Pacific: they aren't afraid to try a variety of locomotives. This motive power scene in 1965 shows Alco, GE and EMD diesels camping out at the diesel facilities. *Chris Burritt*

Apparently used for grander things, this Union Pacific observation car may have once been assigned to the *City of St. Louis, Portland Rose, Butte Special, City of San Francisco* or *City of Portland.* Always passenger-minded, in 1965 UP was still running a mixed train between Columbus and Albion, Nebraska, and from Kearney to Stapleton. Can you believe it? *Chris Burritt*

A study in solidity, this Union Pacific PA was regeared for freight service in 1955, 10 years prior to this picture. The PA's saw passenger service assignments on occasion after that, but in 1965 they were traded in, except for #607. *Chris Burritt*

This was western-state railroading in 1957 on the still-glamorous Union Pacific! #3803 with only the help from her own fire-breathing belly pulls a mile-long freight train over the high iron on September 15. *Charles Zeiler*

With the slogan *Dependable Transportation* its motto, Union Pacific #1141 Alco S4 keeps the passenger varnish on the right track and in the right train. *Chris Burritt*

A profile view of #1171 with its slogan *Road of the Streamliners. Chris Burritt*

186

An E9 with 2,400-hp backs up to couple onto her next passenger train. Union Pacific was the second customer of EMD's to purchase the E9's, finally having 69 on UP property, including 35 A units and 34 B units. Two dozen were rebuilt from old E units. *Chris Burritt*

ABOVE. EMD GP9 #315 is switching cars at North Topeka, Kansas in July of 1978. It was one of the Geep 9's not turbocharged to 2,000-hp. *Bob Nicholson* RIGHT. #X473 is a 2,000-hp GP20, one of 30 units built in 1960 for the UP. *Chris Burritt*

#936 and #938 diesel E units await their turn at heading up the next Union Pacific passenger train on a bright, clear blue-sky morning. *Chris Burritt*

ABOVE. The crew at Denver's Union Station has some time to kill before departure. There's plenty of express mail to be loaded. RIGHT. #934 may have hit something as per the marks on her nose. *Both photos, Chris Burritt*

ABOVE. A GE U25B with 2,500-hp is three years old in this picture. The unit behind is a GP9B; the UP was one of a couple of roads to own GP9B's. *Chris Burritt*

RIGHT. #738B was one of 40 GP30B's built in 1963 for the UP. *Chris Burritt*

Two GP39's and DD35 combined offer 9,500-hp for this train. *Chris Burritt*

Turbine #12 served Union Pacific for nine years. *Chris Burritt*

ABOVE. A close-up view of turbine #12; the unit was built in February 1960 and retired in October of 1969. The turbines developed 7,000-hp on the rail; they could pull 735 fully loaded freight cars on straight, level track. RIGHT. Oil spills mark the tender of 12-12B. Under a full load, the turbine consumed 800 gallons of residual fuel an hour. *Both photos, Chris Burritt*

United States Army

Steam's up at Ft. Eustis, Virginia with this tripleheader passenger excursion. *Brad Smith*

LEFT. The same three U.S. Army locomotives as above, freshly painted. *Brad Smith* RIGHT, TOP. #714, a 0-4-0T at Eustis in August of 1969. *Collection of Don Heimburger* RIGHT, BOTTOM. A Baldwin 4TC at Baraboo, Wisconsin ammunitions plant in 1974. *Brad Smith*

United States Navy

ABOVE. Even the untrained eye can probably see that these two U.S. Navy CC road switchers haven't turned a wheel in a few years. The units are on a Chesapeake & Ohio side track north of Cass, West Virginia on October 14, 1976. *Collection of Don Heimburger*

U.S. Navy switcher #65-00351 is at Quonset Point Naval Air Station in Rhode Island in 1964. *Brad Smith*

Wabash

ABOVE. *Serving the Heart of America*, the Wabash Railroad's Cannon B[all] made direct connections with the Domeliner *City of St. Lou[is]* at St. Lou[is] Delmar Station for Kansas City, Denver and the West. There was only o[ne] change of trains and no change of stations. The Wabash *Cannon Ball* in 19[ ] featured a dining-lounge car and reclining seat chair cars. Leaving St. Lo[uis] daily at 9:15 a.m., the train reached Detroit's Union Station at 8:25 p.m. [a] distance of 488.8 miles. Here the *Cannon Ball* is at Decatur, Illinois on Janua[ry] 8, 1961. *Richard Wallin*

LEFT. Wabash's *Banner Blue* rounding the cut-off at Bement, Illinois in Aug[ust] of 1966. At Bement the Wabash journeyed north to Chicago, east to Detr[oit] and south to St. Louis. *Richard Wallin*

Alco-GE ex-Ann Arbor FA-2 with 1,600-hp sits dead with other Wabash units. Note gray roof. Four of these units came off the Ann Arbor and all were traded to Alco in 1965. *FJC Products*

Wabash #1001 EMD E7A is a 2,000-hp passenger unit; it was one of 14 such diesels ordered from EMD in 1947 and retired in 1965. *FJC Products*

Another E8 in the blue and yellow striped paint scheme was #1008. It could be seen at times pulling the Domeliner *Banner Blue* between St. Louis and Chicago. The *Banner Blue* left St. Louis at 4 p.m. and arrived in Chicago at 9:20 p.m. After a night's sleep, businessmen could make their rounds the following day and catch the *Blue Bird* back at 3:50 p.m., arriving home again at 9:15 p.m. *FJC Products*

LEFT. #598 Fairbanks-Morse 2,350-hp H-24-66 (ex-550) was built for the Wabash in 1954. The six-axle diesels were hefty power for the railroad. After these, the only other Wabash units to arrive were 2,400-hp FM diesels, Alco DL640A's, GE U25B's and EMD GP-35's. *FJC Products*

BELOW, LEFT. Showing its age (built 1953), #721 GMD F7 was one of numerous F7's on the Wabash. BELOW, RIGHT. GP7, FA and another GP7 team up for freight hauling. The Wabash's diesel locomotive roster was fairly simple, although it did include Alco, Baldwin, EMD, GE and FM units. *FJC Products*

Dearborn Station was the Chicago home of the *Blue Bird*, the *Banner Blue* and the *Orland Park*, shown here, a local passenger train that ran between Chicago's downtown and Orland Park, a south suburb. The old Standard Oil Building is in the background. *FJC Products*

ABOVE. With the Norfolk & Western Geep directly behind it, Wabash #452 is no doubt now part of the N&W system. The merger between the Nickel Plate Road, N&W, and Wabash took place on Friday, October 16, 1964. *FJC Products* RIGHT. Freight train at Des Moines, Iowa in 1963. *Charles Zeiler* BELOW. Wabash 1,750-hp GP9. *FJC Products*

Warwick Railway

Originally from the Boston Naval Yard, this Atlas-type 50-ton 300-hp diesel was built in 1938. Before coming to the Warick Railway, it served Ever Ready Supply as their #214. The Warick ran from Cranston to Bellefonte, Rhode Island, a distance of only two miles. *Brad Smith*

Waterloo Railroad

EMD SW900 #3 of the Waterloo Railroad wears a black and white suit similar to big brother Illinois Central which owned it. Date: August of 1965. *Charles Zeiler*

Western Maryland

Western Maryland was a 878-mile line that ran between Baltimore, Maryland and Connellsville, Pennsylvania and into West Virginia to Durbin. The road started to dieselize in 1949, but mostly in the East, away from the coal mines it served. The road offered coach passenger service only. In 1967, the B&O-C&O received permission to control the WM; in 1983, the B&O merged with WM. Above, GP7 #23 was made a chopnose unit in 1973. *Brad Smith* RIGHT. At Elkins, West Virginia in June of 1979, four diesels, including two C&O units, get ready to roll. *Jerry Carson*

Alco #304 FA2, #301, #302 and helpers are at Hagerstown, Maryland on April 4, 1971. By late 1950, WM wanted more road diesels, but EMD was at capacity. The WM instead bought four Alco FA's #301-304. While not like other WM units, the FA's were successful nonetheless. *Jerry Carson*

Western Pacific

Photo by Don Heimburger

Western Pacific Alco S2 works Oakland, California in 1966 along with a mate. The unit was later sold to the Tidewater Southern. The WP began in 1903 but entered into bankruptcy 13 years later. The line was merged with the Union Pacific on December 22, 1981. *Brad Smith*

The Western Pacific was a passenger-conscious line. The *California Zephyr* timetable appeared more like a travel brochure, showing all the spectacular destinations the train ran. *Westbound or eastbound...you enjoy Vista-Dome views of the Colorado Rockies and California's Feather River Canyon during daylight hours,* read the timetable. The *Zephyr* featured five air-conditioned domes, each seating 24 passengers. Here, that famous train glides down the streets of Oakland, California in 1962 (above) and 1966 (right). *Above photo by Richard Wallin; photo at right by Brad Smith*

White Pass & Yukon

White Pass

The three-foot-gauge White Pass & Yukon Railroad operated from the height of the Klondike Gold Rush in 1898 until 1982 when world metal prices plummeted, mines in the Yukon shut down and White Pass operations were suspended. The WP&Y has one of the steepest railroad grades in North America; the line climbs 2,885 feet in 20 miles. The highest point on the system is 2,916 feet at Log Cabin, British Columbia. Of the 110.7 miles of track, 20 percent is in Alaska, 30 percent is in British Columbia and half is in Yukon Territory. Tunnel Mountain on the line is especially spectacular. A General Electric diesel built in 1956 stands shiny and proud at Whitehorse in 1963. *Brad Smith*

Timeless yard limit sign on the Strasburg Railroad in Pennsylvania in July, 1988. *Don Heimburger*

Index